Miss Audery Hepburn

A One-Woman Play
in Two Acts

By

Michael B. Druxman

The Hollywood Legends

© Copyright 2019 by Michael B. Druxman

CAUTION: Professionals and amateurs are hereby warned that *Miss Audrey Hepburn* is an original work and subject to a royalty. It is fully protected under the copyright laws of the United States of America and of all countries with which the United States has reciprocal copyright relations.

All rights, including professional, amateur, motion picture, radio, television, recitation, public reading and the rights of translation into foreign languages are strictly reserved.

All questions with regard to licensing should be addressed to the author: Michael B. Druxman, PMB 119, 4301 W. William Cannon Dr., Suite B-150, Austin, TX 78749 [*druxy@ix.netcom.com*].

No performance of any or all of the play may be given without obtaining in advance the written permission of the author and paying the requisite fee.

TIME

The play is set in 1990 in the Tolochenaz Vaud, Switzerland, home of Audrey Hepburn.

SETTING

The living room of Audrey Hepburn's home in Tolochenaz, Vaud, Switzerland.

The main entry to the home is off-stage, UR; bedrooms and the rest of the house, off-stage UL.

Furnishings are, for the most part, tasteful, modern European: a sofa, armchair, coffee and end tables. Also in the room is a wet bar, with a small mirror atop it.

The house is clean; well-kept.

MISS AUDREY HEPBURN

ACT I

AT RISE: *The stage is empty. After a moment,* AUDREY HEPBURN *(She's in her fifties, but looks years younger.), sweeps into the room from* UL. *She is attired in blouse and slacks. She moves* DC; *speaks to audience, as if she's filming a commercial.*

AUDREY

Hello.

I'm Audrey Hepburn.

I'm here to talk to you about UNICEF.

That's the United Nations International Children's Emergency Fund.

UNICEF was created by the United Nations General Assembly in 1946 to provide emergency food and health care to children and mothers in countries that had been devastated by World War II....

A memory lapse makes her pause for a moment, then:

In 1950, UNICEF's mandate was extended to address the long-term needs of children and women in developing countries everywhere....

> *Again, she pauses, then:*

I'm sorry. Can we take that again?

My mind was wandering.

Whenever I talk about the War...

It brings back memories.
              (*Chuckles*)
I thought I'd gotten over that...

But, they keep creeping back in.
              (*Starts to exit.*)
Do you want to take it from the top?

> *She exits* UL, *then after a few moments, re-enters; crosses* DC.

Hello.

I'm Audrey Hepburn.

I'm here to talk to you about UNICEF....

> *She stops, then:*

Damn!

I don't know what's wrong with me today.

It's close to lunch time. Could we, please, finish this after lunch?

I just need some time to get my head together.

Thank you.

I'll just stay here...and ponder for an hour.

> *She sits on the sofa; lights cigarette, then she speaks to audience:*

Did you see Dickie Attenboough's movie, *A Bridge Too Far*?
> (*Chuckles*)

Sorry. That's Richard Attenborough.

The movie was about the battle of Arnhem.

It had an all-star cast: Robert Redford, Sean Connery, Michael Caine, Laurence Olivier...

They wanted me to be in it, too.

Play Kate ter Horst.

She was a Dutch woman who turned her house outside of Arnhem into a hospital for the Allies.

She's a Dutch national hero.

I couldn't do it.

> *Stands; paces.*

I was in Arnhem during the war.

I couldn't live through that again...even for a movie.

Liv Ullmann did the part and, I know, she was marvelous.

I don't do movies about World War II.

I don't even like to see movies about World War II.

I put all that behind me.

I thought I'd put all that behind me.

My life has gone along....

It's certainly been full...busy....

Theatre...movies...family...

Then, every now and then, a memory of the War pops up, and....

I go up on my lines.

Unfinished business.

That's what they call it: "Unfinished business".

Maybe I should finish it, once and for all.

My cigarette went out.

Lights cigarette.

I smoke three packs a day. I know I shouldn't, but...

Shrugs.

We've got an hour or so before the crew gets back.

You're nice people.

Want to help me through this?

You might learn something about Audrey Hepburn you didn't know before.

I might learn something about Audrey Hepburn I didn't know before.

Crosses to wet bar; pours drink.

You want one?

She sips the drink, then:

I never thought I'd land in pictures with a face like mine.

I was asked to act when I couldn't act.

I was asked to sing and dance with Fred Astaire in *Funny Face* when I couldn't sing and dance and do all kinds of things I wasn't prepared for.

I tried like mad to cope with it.

On top of that, the weather in Paris was terrible.

Fred and I kept slipping on the muddy, wet grass.

Fred wasn't easy.

He was...grumpy.

Here I've been waiting for twenty years to dance with Fred Astaire, and what do I get?

Mud in my eye.

I guess I was no Ginger Rogers.
                (*Chuckles*)
I probably hold the distinction of being the one movie star who, by all laws of logic, should never have made it.

At each stage of my career, I lacked the experience.

If I were to write my autobiography, it would start like this:

I was born in Brussels, Belgium, on May 4, 1929... and I died six weeks later.

I had a severe coughing attack. I turned blue and stopped breathing.

My mother prayed...and spanked my bottom until I came back to life.

A second chance.

Ella, my mother, was of noble descent, a Baroness.

She wanted to be an actress; sing opera...

But, being in "the theatre" would have brought "disgrace" upon the family.
> (*Chuckles*)

I guess I've disgraced my family.

My mother was not a very affectionate person.

She was a fabulous mother, but she had a Victorian upbringing.

She was very strict...very demanding.

Me?

I was never into dolls.

I had a passion for the outdoors: trees...birds...flowers....

And, Rudyard Kipling.
> (*Recites:*)

"*A woman is only a woman, but a good cigar is a smoke.*"
> (*Chuckles:*)

What did you expect me to recite? *Gunga Din*?

All right.... If it will make you happy.
> (*Recites:*)

"*Though I've belted you and flayed you.*
"*By the living God that made you.*
"*You're a better man than I am, Gunga Din.*"

> *She takes a mock half bow.*

Father was Joseph Victor Anthony Hepburn-Ruston.

He was born in Bohemia; of English and Austrian ancestry.

My studio bios speak of him as having been a banker, but he wasn't that at all.

After he married my mother, he handled the family finances, but he never really held down a job.

Truth be told: My father was a Fascist.

A Fascist!

He toured Germany to see what life was like under the Nazis.

He even met Hitler.

My mother went with him, but I don't believe she shared his political views.

She was trying to hold her marriage together.

It didn't help.

I was six-years-old when Father moved out.

It was the most traumatic event in my life.

Mother's hair turned white when he left.

I worshiped my father and missed him terribly from the day he disappeared.

I always envied other girls.

They had a daddy.

> *Lights another cigarette.*

Mother took me to England, and enrolled me in a boarding school.

I was terrified about being away from home.

I was shy...overweight. My English wasn't perfect.

The other girls made fun of me.

My parents' divorce was final in 1938.

Father was somewhere in England, but he didn't try to see me.

I made the school honor roll.

And, I fell in love with dancing.

In this village in Kent where I stayed, there was a young dancer who would come up from London once a week and give ballet lessons.

I loved it; just loved it.

And then, the Nazis invaded Poland.

> PHONE RINGS.

Perfect timing.

What do they call that?

Saved by the bell.

She answers the phone.

Hello?

Yes, this is Miss Hepburn.

I'll hold.
(*To audience:*)
My agent.

I don't know why he keeps calling.

He knows I'm not interested in doing movies any more.

I turned down *40 Carats...Nicholas and Alexandra...The Exorcist...One Flew over the Cuckoo's Nest....*

I could have won an Oscar for that one. Louise Fletcher did.

The film I really wanted to do was *The Turning Point.*

I could have played a ballet dancer.

But, they cast Anne Bancroft.

Actually, I preferred retirement; staying home and being with my sons.
(*Into phone:*)
Hello?

I'm doing well.

We're just filming a commercial for UNICEF.

You know, I'm not interested in doing another movie.

I don't care who's directing....

Spielberg!?!

Steven Spielberg?

I loved *E.T.*

I love all his films.

Ten days work?

So, it's not the lead.

It's a "cameo".

I don't think...

A million dollars for ten days work!?!

Steven must really want me.

Okay, I will read the script...but no promises.

Talk to you soon.

> *She hangs up the phone.*

They're going to shoot the picture in Montana.
(*Chuckles*)

I don't think they'll have me wearing any Givenchy gowns in Montana.

A million dollars for ten days work.

You've come a long way, Audrey.

Givenchy?

His are the only clothes in which I am myself.

He created "*The Hepburn Look*":

Spare, simple lines...dominant black and whites....

I depend on Givenchy in the same way that American women depend on their psychiatrist.

So, where were we?

That's right. Hitler had invaded Poland.

Britain declared war on Germany...

And, Mother insisted I leave school, and come back to Arnhem.

England could be bombed at any time, and Holland was neutral.

Or, so we thought.

And, father?

Somehow Mother had contacted him and asked him to meet me at the train in London where I was coming in from Kent.

They put me on this plane, and it flew very low. It was one of the last planes out.

That was the last time I saw my father.

We didn't know it at the time, but....

He was imprisoned by the British for the duration of the war.

He was pro-Nazi.

Back in Arnhem...

I was eleven.

I had an enormous complex about my looks. I thought I was ugly, and I thought nobody would ever marry me.

But, I still loved ballet.

I took classes at the Arnhem School of Music under Winja Marova, who claimed to be a former Russian ballerina.

I lost weight...

Winja was the first dancer I really got to know.

She helped this very young girl to believe that she could become one, too.

I was going to be a ballerina! I was very fanatic about it.

She refreshes her drink; downs it.

In May of 1940, I was fortunate enough to attend a performance of The Sadler's Wells Ballet.

I was so excited.

For the occasion, my mother had our little dressmaker make me a long taffeta dress.

I'd never had a long dress in my life.

You see, at the end of the performance, I was to present a bouquet of flowers to the director of the company.

I remember that night very well.

Not so much about what happened on stage, but later than night, the Germans invaded Holland.

They wanted to use the Dutch airfields to bomb France and England and to support their own troops.

All civilians were ordered to remain indoors, and not look out the windows.

Naturally, we peeked.

There was no fighting.

Just the grey uniforms of the German soldiers, and the rumble of trucks.

They took complete charge of the town.

The Germans tried to be civil and to win our hearts.

The first few months, we didn't know quite what had happened.

A child is a child is a child.

I just went to school...

And, I avoided speaking English.

I used the name "Edda van Heemstra".

I didn't want to end up in a concentration camp.

I'd go to the station with my mother to take a train, and I'd see cattle trucks filled with Jews...

Families with little children, with babies, herded into meat wagons.

All the nightmares I've ever had are mingled with that.

> *She pauses; wipes a tear from her eye, then:*

We saw young men put against the wall and shot.

Don't discount anything awful you hear or read about the Nazis.

It was worse than you could ever imagine.

My Uncle Otto: He was executed in retaliation for an act of sabotage by the resistance movement.

He had nothing to do with the act, but he was targeted because of his family's prominence in Dutch society.

I did what little I could.

I gave underground dance concerts to raise money for the resistance.

I took a message to the underground, so that they could rescue a downed Allied flyer who was hiding in the woods.

Once I had to step in and deliver our tiny underground newspaper. I stuffed them in my woolen socks in my wooden shoes, got on my bike and delivered them.

We lived with my grandfather.

He became the father figure in my life.

I adored him.

He and I would do very old crossword puzzles, sitting around a little lamp with no heat.

Had we known that we were going to be occupied for five years, we might have all shot ourselves.

We thought it might be over next week...six months...next year....

That's how we got through.

There may have been a war, but your dreams for yourself go on, and I wanted to be a dancer.

After D-Day, living conditions got worse.

In September of 1944, the Allies launched "*Operation Market Garden*".

That was *A Bridge To Far.*

It failed.

Arnhem was heavily damaged.

There was famine.

The Germans blocked the resupply routes in retaliation for the railway strikes that were held to hinder the German occupation.

Our family resorted to making flour out of tulip bulbs, so we could bake cakes and biscuits.

I developed anemia... respiratory problems... jaundice... edema....

I was five-foot-six, and weighted ninety pounds.

Malnutrition will do that to you.

I was sixteen when the war ended...

The Allied troops marched into Arnhem.

They gave us chocolate bars...lots of chocolate bars.

I ate them, and became violently ill.
>(*Chuckles*)

Too much, too soon.

The UNRRA...the forerunner to UNICEF... filled the schools with boxes of food that we were allowed to take home...and blankets, medication and clothes...

Beautiful clothes.

It was everything we dreamed of.

Our family had lost everything due to the war: Our houses... our possessions... our money...

But, we didn't give a hoot.

We got through it with our lives, which was all that mattered.

We moved to Amsterdam.

Ella worked as a cook and housekeeper for a wealthy family....

And, I took up ballet again, studying under Sonia Gaskell and Olga Tarasova.

I wanted to wear a tutu and dance at Covent Garden.

That was my dream, but not my plan.

I never thought I'd make it.

Actually, because of the war, I was now a little too old to become a ballerina, but I could become a choreographer.

Mother's dream was for me to marry a rich man, so we could return to the lifestyle we had before the war.

We didn't share the same dream.

I was nineteen.

I wanted to go to London. There were more opportunities there.

I had a British passport...a scholarship for the Marie Rambert Ballet School...but no money for living expenses.

Marie Rambert would have to wait.

In Amsterdam, I did modeling; played a stewardess in a movie travelogue.

And, in 1948, mother and I were finally able to move to England.

We were delighted to be in London.

To be able to buy a pair of shoes when you wanted to, or to take a taxi when you wanted...

We only took taxis when it rained.

Most times, we rode the underground.

But, I did go on an eating binge.

I would eat everything in sight and in any quantity.

I'd empty a jam jar in one sitting with a spoon.

I became quite tubby and put on twenty pounds.

And then, I went on a ruthless diet and lost thirty pounds.

I was studying ballet with Marie Rambert...

And, I'd pick up extra money by modeling. I even modeled with Roger Moore.

That was long before he was James Bond.

I never heard from my father, or knew anything about him during the war.

But, after the war, curiosity took over.

I wanted to know where he was; whether he was still alive.

Through the Red Cross, I found that he lived in Ireland.

But, it took me years before I could write to him; before I could say, "I want to see you."

Maybe I was afraid to see him.

I also picked up extra money by dancing in shows on London's West End.

I was in the London production of *High Button Shoes*.

I had one line.

People said they could hardly hear me, so I took some singing and elocution lessons.

One of my instructors was Felix Aylmer, that wonderful character actor who had played "Polonius" in Laurence Olivier's film of *Hamlet*.

He taught me to concentrate intelligently on what I was doing, and made me aware that all actors need a "method" of sorts to be even vaguely professional.

There were more parts in films.

Small parts, like cigarette girls.

If you look quickly, you'll spot me in *The Lavender Hill Mob* with Alec Guinness.

Alec liked me, and he recommended me to Mervyn LeRoy, who was in London casting *Quo Vadis*.

LeRoy tested me, but I was too thin and Deborah Kerr got the part.

Everything significant in my life has happened gloriously and unexpectedly.

I was on the Riviera, doing a small role in a film, *Monte Carlo Baby*.

And, who should spot me, but Colette, the author of *Gigi*.

"That's my Gigi," she said.

They were looking for an actress to play "Gigi" on Broadway.

"I wouldn't be able to play Gigi," I told her. "I've only done small parts. I can't act."

Of course, I got the part and went to New York.

There were so many times during rehearsals that Gilbert Miller, the producer, wanted to fire me.

I didn't know how to project.

I didn't know how to make an entrance.

Cathleen Nesbitt, who played "Aunt Alicia," said that I'd come bounding out onto the stage like a gazelle.

I'd told them I couldn't act.

The only thing that saved me was that it was too close to opening to recast my part.

Wonderful Cathleen Nesbitt took me under her wing.

When we weren't rehearing...night, day, weekends... she coached me through it.

Our first preview was in Philadelphia in November of 1951.

It was a disaster.

Right at the climax, I forgot my lines and everything stopped.

But, I managed to pull round and last until the final curtain.

Mr. Miller wanted to either replace me or close the show.

How could you blame him?

Then, the reviews came out.

They were raves.
                    (*Incredulous*)
Once paper said I was "*the acting find of the year*".

Another said I was "*as fresh and frisky as a puppy out of a tub.*"

On the other hand, Noel Coward came backstage to tell me something he found wrong with my performance.

He said I was "*rather too noisy*".

I was terribly flattered.

(*Ponders, then:*)

Gigi was a hit!

I was a hit!

Colette sent me an autographed photo: "*For Audrey Hepburn, a treasure that I found on the sands.*"

And then, another miracle happened.

Actually, it happened before I went to New York...

I was preparing to do *Gigi* when William Wyler saw one of the little films I'd made.

I had no idea who William Wyler was; no sense of what he could do for my career.

I had no sense period.

I was awfully new and awfully young, and thrilled just to be going out on auditions and meeting people who seemed to like me.

I did a screen test for Wyler at Pinewood Studios in London.

I guess I did okay, because he offered me the part.

I tried to explain to him that I wasn't ready for a leading role.

But, he didn't agree and I certainly wasn't going to argue with him.

He was even willing to delay filming until *Gigi* closed.

Paramount did ask me to change my last name.

They didn't want people to confuse me with Katharine Hepburn.

How could anybody confuse me with Katharine Hepburn?

They also wanted a seven-year contract, but I balked at that, too.

They settled for two years.

Oh, by the way, the name of the movie I tested for was *Roman Holiday*...but you probably already knew that.

I played a runaway princess, and my leading man was Gregory Peck.

Gregory Peck!

In one of the final scenes, I had to cry.

I had no idea how to come by those tears.

The night was getting longer and longer, and Willie Wyler was waiting.

Out of the blue, he came over and gave me hell.

"*We can't stay here all night,*" he said. "*Can't you cry, for God's sake?*"

He'd never spoken to me like that, ever, during the picture. He'd been so nice and gentle.

I broke into such sobs, and he shot the scene, and that was it.

Afterwards he said, "*I'm sorry, but I had to get you to do it somehow.*"

Gregory Peck was so kind.

He insisted that I get equal billing with him on the picture.

"*You might as well,*" he said. "*You're going to steal the picture anyway.*"

Immediately after we finished filming, I went back to the United States and did the national company of *Gigi*.

We played Boston, Detroit, Washington, Los Angeles.

And, I broke off my engagement.

Oh! I didn't tell you about that, did I?

I was engaged to James Hanson... Lord Hanson.

I could have been Lady Hanson.

I had a wedding gown, and all the plans had been made.

Jimmy was even willing to let me do a play or a movie every year, but that wouldn't be a career...

And, with *Gigi* a hit and *Roman Holiday* in the can, I was on the brink of a major career.

I'd worked so hard. How could I give that up?

Besides, my mother didn't want me to get married, and neither did Paramount.

Jimmy and I are still good friends.

I've never wanted for beaus.

I've even gone out to dinner with Groucho Marx.

He was sixty-two years old.
                     (*Chuckles*)
He told the press that I was too old and wrinkled for him.

There were even rumors about me and Gregory Peck, which was ridiculous.

I'm not a home breaker.

I was in London for the opening of *Roman Holiday*, and Greg was there making another picture.

He invited me to a party, and that's where I first met Mel Ferrer.

He was a talented actor...director...

I'd loved him in *Lili*, the movie he'd made with Leslie Caron.

He was in England filming *Knights of the Round Table* with Robert Taylor and Ava Gardner. He was playing "King Arthur".

The way he looked me in the eyes...

He just penetrated me with his eyes.

I think I fell in love with him then...

Or, did I fall in love with the character he played in *Lili*?

I went back to the United States and did a movie for Billy Wilder: *Sabrina* with Humphrey Bogart and William Holden.

It was supposed to be Cary Grant and William Holden, but Cary dropped out at the last moment.

Bogie didn't like being second choice, even if they were paying him a lot of money.

I was rather terrified of him, and he knew it.

He'd make remarks.

So, what if I did have to do several takes for each scene.

We had to get it right, didn't we?

I had to get it right.

I think Bogie also resented the fact that I was having a bit of a romance with Bill Holden while we were filming.

They'd done a picture together years before, and they hadn't gotten along.

A lot of people didn't get along with Bogie.

Bill said he was going to leave his wife for me.

And then, he told me that he'd had a vasectomy, and that ended it.

When I married, I wanted to have children.

Ponders, then:

Mel Ferrer sent me a play.

It was *Ondine* by Jean Giraudoux.

I'd play a water sprite.

I loved it.

How often do you get the opportunity to play a water sprite?

They were going to pay me $2500 per week plus a percentage of the gross, which was a vast improvement over the $500 per week I got for doing *Gigi*.

Alfred Lunt was directing, and, Mel would be my co-star.

I insisted on that

After all, he'd brought me the project. I even insisted that he get half of my percentage of the gross.

I know, but...

I didn't have a business advisor then.

The rehearsals for *Ondine* were not...peaceful.

Mel and Lunt did not get along.

Mel didn't like the way he was directing me.

We were a couple by that time, and I was caught in the middle.

I don't like being caught in the middle.

Opening night, Mel and I took a joint curtain call.

Actually, when I stepped out to take my bow, he stepped out with me.

He made a speech; thanked Alfred Lunt for his direction.

Later, at the cast party, Lunt said Mel was a *"horse's ass"*.

That wasn't very nice.

Other people in the company also felt the same way, but I was in love with him.

On his thirty-seventh birthday, I gave him a Rolex watch.

I had it engraved: *"Mad About the Boy"*.

We both liked Noel Coward.

In spite of everything, *Ondine* was a hit.

Roman Holiday had just been released a week or so before we opened, so I'm sure that helped.

It certainly helped when, a month after we opened, I won the Oscar.

I was so surprised when they called my name that I didn't know what to do.

And, three days later, I won the Tony Award for *Ondine*.

I couldn't believe it!

I was chosen over Deborah Kerr in *Tea and Sympathy*...Geraldine Page in *The Immoralist*.... Margaret Sullavan in *Sabrina Fair*.

I felt badly about Margaret. After all, she'd originated the role in *Sabrina* that I'd just finished playing in the movie.

I was twenty-four years old.

I'd only been in show business for six years .

And now, I had an Oscar and a Tony Award.

How would I ever live up to them?

It was like being given something when you were a child; something too big for you that you must grow into.

Ondine closed after three months.

I was exhausted; losing weight...smoking too much.

I'd gone from *Gigi* into *Roman Holiday* back into *Gigi*, then into *Sabrina* and into *Ondine*.

Mel and I flew to Switzerland for a vacation, and that's when he asked me to marry him.

Mother wasn't too happy about that.

Mel had been married three times before; twice to the same woman.

He had children.

But, I married him on the shores of Lake Lucerne on September 24, 1954.

We made our home in Switzerland

After that, life became much more interesting.

> *She reacts to something OS, then to audience:*

The crew is back.

And, I haven't even gotten my head together.

I guess we'll have to finish this later.

> *She crosse* UL, *as:*
>
> LIGHTS FADE.

END OF ACT I

ACT II

> AT RISE: *A packed suitcase and an overnight bag are by the front door. Audrey enters from* UL, *carrying her purse. She wears a skirt and blouse. She puts her purse down on the suitcase; checks her watch, then moves* DS.

AUDREY
(*To Audience:*)
The car isn't going to be here for awhile, so we have time to finish our talk.

Sorry it's taken so long, but a lot has happened since we last saw each other.

I'm doing another trip for UNICEF.

I've been to Ethiopia...South America,,,Bangladesh...

This time, I'm going to Vietnam.

We want to get the Vietnamese government to cooperate with our immunization and clean water programs.

The "Third World" is a term I don't like very much because we're all one world.

I want people to know that the largest part of humanity is suffering.

When Audrey Hepburn travels for UNICEF there's a lot of publicity, and things get done.
          (*Ponders, then:*)
Where were we when we left off last time?

I did do the Spielberg movie. It wasn't a large role, but it was fun.

It was a reworking of an old picture that starred Spencer Tracy, Irene Dunne and Lionel Barrymore: *A Guy Named Joe*.

It's called *Always*.

Richard Dreyfuss and Holly Hunter are the stars...

And, I'm playing the Lionel Barrymore part.
          (*She starts to explain, then:*)
Don't ask.

Just see the movie when it's released. You'll understand.

          She pours herself a drink.

Shortly after Mel and I married, I got pregnant...

I was so happy.

And then, I had a miscarriage.

The first of several.

After that, Mel and I did *War and Peace* together for Dino De Laurentiis.

41

Dino signed Mel first, probably because he knew that, if Mel was doing the movie, he'd get me to play "*Natasha*".

Mel got a hundred thousand for doing the picture.

I got three hundred-fifty thousand.

What difference did it make?

We were married, weren't we?

Mel made sure my costumes were right; that my car was there on time....

Other people on the production were annoyed with him, but...

He took care of me.

"*Natasha*" was the toughest role I ever did.

I did *War and Peace* in velvets and furs in August.

In the hunting scene where I'm in velvet and a high hat, we're plodding across this big field in the blazing sunshine and, all of a sudden, my horse fainted out from under me.

Not the last time I had a problem with a horse.

They got me out of the saddle, and I didn't end up being rolled over.

So, when they say I'm strong as a horse, I am.

I'm stronger!

I didn't faint. The horse did.

Dino was hoping that *War and Peace* would be the next *Gone With the Wind*.

It had me...Mel...Henry Fonda in the cast, and it was certainly long enough.

But, it was released the same year as *The Ten Commandments* and *Around the World in Eighty Days*.

The critics didn't like it, particularly Henry Fonda.

He's a great actor, but *War and Peace* is set in Russia, and Henry's as American as you can get.

After *War and Peace*, I did *Funny Face* with Fred Astaire...*Love in the Afternoon* with Gary Cooper....

Did you ever notice how I always seemed to get cast opposite men who are old enough to be my father?

Who cares how old they were?

They were Humphrey Bogart. Fred Astaire...Gary Cooper....

Anyone who doesn't like it can go jump in the lake.

On the other hand, Maurice Chevalier played my father in *Love in the Afternoon*

He was delightful.

Maybe it might have been more credible if he and Coop had switched roles.
>(*Chuckles, then:*)

George Stevens offered me *The Diary of Anne Frank*.

A friend had given me the book in 1946 in galley form.

I read it...and it destroyed me.

Anne's story was my own.

I've never been quite the same again, it affected me so deeply.

Otto Frank, Anne's father, came to my home in Switzerland to try to talk me into taking the role.

He was remarried...to another survivor.

He struck me as somebody who's been purged by fire. There was something so spiritual about his face

He had been there and back.

I couldn't do the film.

I didn't want to exploit Anne Frank's life and death to my advantage - to get another salary...to be praised in a movie.

Besides, I was too old for the part.

I couldn't play a fifteen-year old.

I was offered the role of Maria von Trapp, which I also turned down for pretty much the same reason.

I didn't want to do a movie that had Nazis in it.

And, it's a good thing that I didn't do it.

If I had done that picture, we might never have had *The Sound of Music*.

So, what movie did I do?

The Nun's Story.

I tried to get Mel into it, but the director, Fred Zinnemann, wasn't interested.

He cast Peter Finch.

I did try.

The film was shot on location in Rome, Bruges, Stanleyville and a real leper colony in the Congo.

My arm was so sore from all the shots I had to take.

It's a good thing I got the shots. I got bitten by a monkey when I was there.

I met the real "Sister Like" while I was preparing for the role.

She was the inspiration for the novel and the film.

We became great friends.

The Nun's Story was an exhausting, 132 day shoot.

When we finished filming in Africa and got back to Rome, I developed the most excruciating pain in my back...

I vomited....

I had a kidney stone. The doctor gave me pills; told me to rest.

Zinnemann shot around me until I was feeling better.

Someone said that kidney ailments were even more painful than childbirth.

So, I was perfectly prepared to have a dozen children.

Even one.

I guess *The Nun's Story* was a trend setter.

So many nuns left their various orders in the decade following the movie's release.

I got another Oscar nomination for *The Nun's Story*.

By the way: Contrary to reports in the gossip columns, I did not demand that a bidet be provided for me while we were on location in the Congo.

How could you hook one up there anyway?

Right after I finished *The Nun's Story*, I began work on *Green Mansions* with Anthony Perkins.

I played "Rima, the Bird Girl," a jungle princess.

I know, it wasn't a typical Audrey Hepburn part, but with me in the picture, it got made... and Mel got to direct.

Good wives support their husbands...even if they don't always agree with their direction.

Most of the crew didn't agree with his direction either.

Green Mansions was a box-office disaster, and Mel never directed another film.

The Unforgiven was my first...and last Western.

We shot it in Mexico.

I increased my smoking habit to sixty cigarettes a day while we were filming that picture.

Nerves.

Burt Lancaster was in the cast, as was Audie Murphy ...Lillian Gish...

John Huston was the director.

That's the film where I fell off a horse and broke my back.

I finished the picture in a brace.

I guess horses don't like me.

It was around this time that my mother wrote to tell me that my father had died.

I was so distraught.

I couldn't bear the idea that I would never see him again.

Mel did some checking, and he found out that it wasn't true.

My father was a alive, and still living in Ireland.

He had never tried to reach me, nor did he ever want to see me.

It's hard for children who are dumped.

I hadn't seen him since the beginning of the war.

But, I had this great need now...to confront him, so I went to Dublin.

He was living in a tiny apartment; just two rooms.

He looked the way I remembered him. Older, yes, but just the same.

He'd seen all my movies.

He said he'd stayed out of my life because he was afraid that his fascist politics and time in prison might hurt my career.
> (*To herself:*)

He'd seen all my movies, but he hadn't seen me.
> (*To audience:*)

I sent him a monthly check; took care of his needs for the rest of his life.

It helped me exorcize the ghost I'd been living with.

> *Ponders, then chuckles:*

Exorcize.

I'm jumping ahead for a moment, but did you know that Bill Friedkin offered me the lead in *The Exorcist*?

I was tempted, but I had two sons then....

That's right: two sons.

I told him that, if he'd shoot the film in Rome where I was living, I'd do it. But, they filmed it in Washington D.C.

They cast Ellen Burstyn, who was terrific.

Okay, now I will tell you about my sons and how I was living in Rome.

But, in chronological order.

I had another miscarriage, but then I got pregnant again and, this time, I was determined not to do any film work.

Nothing was going to jeopardize this child.

I stayed home; knitted baby clothes.

Sean was born in Lucerne on January 17, 1960.

Sean is an Irish form of "*Ian*". It means "*Gift of God*".

With the baby, I felt I had everything a wife could wish for.

But, it's not enough for a man.

It was not enough for Mel.

He couldn't live with himself just being Audrey Hepburn's husband.

And then, I did *Breakfast at Tiffany's*, the jazziest role of my career.

I'm an introvert. Playing an extroverted girl like "Holly Golighty" was the hardest thing I ever did.

Truman Capote, who wrote the novel, didn't think I was right for the part.

He wanted Marilyn Monroe.

Other people thought it was a bit daring for me to play a call girl.

But, didn't you love the little black dress that Givenchy designed for me?

I got to sing in *Breakfast at Tiffany's*: "*Moon River*".

Henry Mancini wrote it especially for me.

Would you believe that some stupid Paramount studio executive wanted to cut that song from the picture.

I told him: "*Over my dead body!*"

As you can see, I'm still here and the song is in the picture.

I did another film for William Wyler, *The Children's Hour*.

Shirley MacLaine and I were accused of being lesbians.

There was another picture with Bill Holden. We shot it in Paris.

He said he was still in love with me, but he was drinking much more than he had been when we'd done *Sabrina*.

The gossip columnists were having a field day, suggesting things about us that weren't true..

One night, Bill smashed up his car....

>*(Ponders, then:)*

I'm sorry. I'd prefer not to talk about *Paris When It Sizzles*.

It was not a happy experience.

Except, the Givenchy gowns were gorgeous.

While I was in Paris, Mel was in Madrid, doing *The Fall of the Roman Empire*.

There were reports of him being seen out with other women, but...

>*(Ponders, then:)*

And then, I finally got to do a movie with Cary Grant.

I'd wanted to work with him ever since he'd backed out of *Sabrina*.

The movie was *Charade*, a light, Hitchcock-like thriller, directed by Stanley Donen.

I'd never met Cary, so Stanley arranged for the three of us to have dinner together..

I was so nervous.

I accidentally knocked over a bottle of red wine, and it spilled over Cary's cream-colored suit.

I was so humiliated, but Cary just removed his jacket, and pretended, very convincingly, that the stain would simply go away. He was so dear about it.

Working with Cary was easy. He did all the acting, and I just reacted.

One day, while we were sitting next to each other, waiting for the next shot, he said to me: "*You've got to learn to like yourself a little more.*"

I've often thought about that.

If I liked myself more, maybe I wouldn't be as tolerant of people who take advantage of my passive nature.

Like Mel.

Peace at any price?

                      PHONE RINGS

Hepburn answers it.

Hello?

Hello, Michael.
      (*To audience:*)
Michael Tilson Thomas.
      (*Into phone:*)
I'm fine. I'm getting ready to leave for Vietnam.

What's up?

I don't have any plans yet for 1997. That's a few years from now.

I'd love to do it, but why don't you ask me in 1996?

Well, pencil me in.

Pencil, not ink.

I'll talk to you soon.

She hangs up; speaks to audience:

Michael and I have been doing these live concerts in Philadelphia...London....for UNICEF.

I read sections from *The Diary of Anne Frank*, and he conducts his original orchestral work that uses themes from the *Kaddish*.

That's the Jewish mourner's prayer.

I know, I couldn't do the movie, but I'm not playing "Anne Frank" here.

I'm just reading from her diary....

I'm just reading from her diary.

It's still not easy, but it's for UNICEF.

Where were we?

My Fair Lady.

Jack Warner had paid Lerner and Lowe over five million dollars for the rights to the musical, and he wanted major stars in it to insure his investment.

Rex Harrison was not a major *film* star, so Warner offered the role of "Henry Higgins" to Cary Grant.
                    (*Chuckles*)
Not only did Cary turn him down, but he also told Warner that if Rex Harrison didn't do the film, he wouldn't go see it.

I desperately wanted to play "Eliza Doolitte," but I knew that, in all fairness, the role belonged to Julie Andrews, who had originated it on Broadway.

I'm a very fair person...even if it's not to my best interest.

Warner didn't want Julie. She hadn't made *Mary Poppins* yet, and she was not a name known to the movie-going public.

I learned that if I turned down the part, Warner would have offered it to another movie actress, and I was as entitled to do it as much as a third girl, so I accepted.

The press wasn't very kind to me. They said I'd "stolen" the role from Julie Andrews.

That's wasn't true, but I guess it made good copy.

I don't think that Rex Harrison was too happy with me either, particularly after he found out that my salary for *My Fair Lady* was four times what he was getting.

But, I was going to sing in a movie.

Not just one song, like "*Moon River*, but "*I Could Have Danced All Night,*" "*Wouldn't It be Loverly,*" and more.

I worked for weeks with a vocal coach. I thought I was doing fine.

Then, George Cukor, the director, took me aside and told me:

Marni Nixon was going to do my singing for me.

Her voice was more suitable for the role.

I was so upset, I walked off the set.

I'd never done that before.

Next day, I came back and apologized for being so wicked.

My Fair Lady swept the Academy Awards that year: Best Picture...Best Director.... Best Actor...

I presented the award to Rex.

I wasn't nominated.

Maybe it was a backlash because I "stole" the role from Julie Andrews, or maybe it was because Marni Nixon did my singing for me.

But, Julie Andrews won the Best Actress award for *Mary Poppins*, and that was a good thing.

You know what she said?

"*My thanks to Jack L. Warner, who made all this possible.*"
                    (*Chuckles*)
Making *My Fair Lady* was exhausting.

It didn't help my home life.

I was starring in the most important picture of the year, and Mel was...just there.

He wasn't pleasant to the people on the set, and they didn't like him.

Jack Warner tried to help out.

He gave Mel a part in *Sex and the Single Girl*, which was shooting on the next soundstage.

Tony Curtis, Natalie Wood and Henry Fonda were the leads, but it kept Mel occupied for awhile.

I tried to ignore the stories about him and other women.

After *My Fair Lady*, I decided to stay home in Switzerland for awhile; take care of my husband and son.

William Wyler came to me again with *How to Steal a Million*.

It was going to shoot in Paris, and Peter O'Toole was my co-star.

>   (*Chuckles*)
Peter got me tipsy one night.

It was cold, and it was just one shot of brandy to warm me up.

Then, I did a scene where I had to drive off in a car. I took a couple of the big set lamps with me.

In *Two For the Road*, I did my first nude scene.

Semi-nude scene.

You get to see the top half of my bare back.

I loved working with Albert Finney.

We spent a lot of time together.
>   (*Ponders, then:*)
As a character says in that movie: "*There's no such thing as permanence any more.*"

I still wanted to save my marriage...even though there were these ongoing rumors about Mel and a Spanish dancer.

He denied them, of course.

Then, he read *Wait Until Dark*.

It was a play by Frederick Knott, who'd written *Dial M. For Murder*.

Lee Remick had done it on Broadway.

She'd played a blind woman being terrorized by three con-man who are after some heroin that is hidden in a doll.

It was a terrific thriller, and playing a blind woman would be a wonderful challenge.

I took lessons on how to be blind: Moving around a room...filling a teakettle...

I learned to judge a person's distance by their voice; to put on make-up without a mirror...

I wore contact lenses in some scenes.

Alan Arkin and Richard Crenna were in the movie, and I got my last Oscar nomination.

Since Mel had found the project, it was only fair that he be allowed to produce *Wait Until Dark*.

We called a temporary truce...

Though I'm sure he had fun auditioning all those models to play a dead body for a two minute bit in the picture.

Mel could be so cold.

I'm sorry he was unhappy, but was it my fault that I was a bigger star than him?

I was tired of making movies anyway.

I wanted to stay home; raise our son.

After *Wait Until Dark*, I quit movies...

I figured that Mia Farrow would get my parts.

And, I also quit Mel.

We got a divorce.

Maybe it was time to stop looking for a father substitute.

A year later, I married Andrea Dotti.

I know. It was quick.

I guess I was used to being part of a couple.

I'd met him on a yacht.

He was a psychiatrist; an assistant professor at the University of Rome.

He was also nine years younger than me.

He charmed me.

Maybe being married to Audrey Hepburn would help his career.

I know that was mean, but...

A year after we were married, Luca was born.

Unfortunately, Andrea was a playboy.

Part of the time we lived in Switzerland. Part of the time we lived in Rome.

When we were in different cities...or sometimes when we were in the same city...there'd be reports...pictures in the newspaper even... that he'd been seen at a nightclub with other women.

I couldn't fulfill his needs, or maybe I didn't know how.

I couldn't fulfill Mel's needs either.

Frankly, I think sex is overrated.

> *Lights cigarette.*

After eight years, I decided to make another film: *Robin and Marian*.

Sean Connery was "Robin Hood" and I was "Maid Marian".

We were playing them...in their later years.

We shot it in Spain...in thirty-six days...eight or nine pages a day..

I'd never worked that fast before.

> *Paces, then:*

I did a couple of movies with Ben Gazzara.

I liked Ben.

There were rumors in the press that we were having an affair.

I didn't say a word, but if Andrea read about it, it would serve him right.

I don't think he really cared.

For our son, I tried to keep our marriage together.

One can only accept so much.

Divorce is one of the worst experiences a human being can go through.

I tried desperately to avoid it...twice.

Marriage should only be one thing: two people decide they love each other so much they want to stay together.

So, if some way I don't fulfill what he needs in a woman - emotionally, physically, sexually, or whatever it is - and he needs somebody else, then I can't stick around.

I'm not the kind to stay and make scenes.

Pours drink.

While I was still married to Andrea, I was in Los Angeles; the houseguest of Connie Wald.

Connie was the widow of producer Jerry Wald.

He produced everything from *An Affair to Remember* to *Peyton Place*.

Connie threw a small dinner party for me, and one of the guests was Robert Wolders, an actor who had had a television series, *Laredo*.

He was also the widower of Merle Oberon, who had died a couple of months before.

He was seven years younger than me....

Hey, I'm doing better. Andrea was nine years younger.

I was charmed with Robert that night, but he didn't register that much.

He was getting over the death of Merle, and, with what was going on with Andrea, it was the worst period in my life, one of the low ebbs.

We both cried into our beers.

Four months later, we met in New York for drinks...for pasta.

Robert was also from Holland.

He was four years old during the war.

We shared many of the same experiences.

I divorced Andrea in 1982.

Robert and I were a couple by then, but there was no need to marry.

We are happy as we are.

I love Robbie very, very much.

It's not *Romeo and Juliet*; we've had our tiffs, but very few.

It's a wonderful friendship; we like each other.

I can trust him. He's absolutely there for me.

> *Looks out window.*

And now, the car is there for me, too.

So, we've spent this time together....

What have we learned?

What have I learned?

I was born with an enormous need for affection, and a terrible need to give it.

People, like my father, even more than things, have to be restored, renewed, revived, reclaimed and redeemed.

Never throw out anyone...unless they're a husband.
    (*Chuckles*)
The most important thing is to enjoy your life - to be happy.

It's all that matters.

DOORBELL RINGS.

As she crosses UR *toward entry.*

If I'm honest, I have to tell you I still read fairy-tales, and I like them best of all.

She exits UR.

LIGHTS FADE TO BLACK.

NARRATOR (*V.O.*)
After a trip to Somalia in 1992 for UNICEF, Audrey Hepburn was diagnosed with abdominal cancer.

She was 63 when she died at her home in Switzerland on January 20, 1993.

AUDREY (*V.O.*)
People keep asking me to write my memoirs.

I don't want to relive it, nor do I need the psychotherapy.

Get on with it!

THE END

THE HOLLYWOOD LEGENDS is a series of one and two-person, two-act plays by Hollywood biographer, historian, screenwriter and playwright Michael B. Druxman that explore the life and times of some of filmdom's most glittering personalities.

From Clara Bow, "The 'It' Girl" of the silent era, through the birth of the talkies with Al Jolson and Maurice Chevalier, on through the thirties and forties with superstars like Clark Gable, Spencer Tracy, Carole Lombard, Errol Flynn, Basil Rathbone, Jeanette MacDonald and Nelson Eddy, Yvonne De Carlo, Gary Cooper, Dick Powell, and, finally, Hollywood's "boy genius," Orson Welles, these anecdote-filled dramatic pieces present a humorous, often touching portrait of each star and the era in which he/she lived.

The collection has now been expanded to include multiple character plays like *LANA & JOHNNY WERE LOVERS*, *SEXY REXY* (Rex Harrison). *B MOVIE*, which deals with the Franchot Tone/ Barbara Payton/Tom Neal scandal of the 1950s, ROBINSON & RAFT, *THE LAST MONSTERS*, *AVA & HER GUYS* (Ava Gardner, plus Mickey Rooney, Arite Shaw and Frank Sinatra) and *CLOWNS ON THE GROUND* (Milton Berle, Joe E. Brown and Bert Lahr).

The plays, many of which have seen several productions, utilize simple costumes and props, and are designed to be staged on a single setting, with shifts in lighting to denote changes in time and place.

All questions with regard to licensing should be addressed to the author: Michael B. Druxman, PMB 119, 4301 W. William Cannon Dr., Suite B-150, Austin, TX 78749 [*druxy@ix.netcom.com*].

Made in the USA
Columbia, SC
21 November 2024